14.20

DATE DUE

SEP 2 7 1999	
NOV 8 = 1999	
DEC 6 - 2000	
MAY 9 - 2002	
JAN 0 4 2005	
FEB 0 7 2005	
JAN 0 3 2006	
MAY 3 1 2008	

DEMCO, INC. 38-2931

The United States

Connecticut

Anne Welsbacher
ABDO & Daughters

visit us at
www.abdopub.com

Published by Abdo & Daughters, 4940 Viking Drive, Suite 622, Edina, Minnesota 55435.
Copyright © 1998 by Abdo Consulting Group, Inc., Pentagon Tower, P.O. Box 36036, Minneapolis, Minnesota 55435 USA. International copyrights reserved in all countries. No part of this book may be reproduced in any form without written permission from the publisher.

Printed in the United States.

Cover and Interior Photo credits: SuperStock, Peter Arnold, Inc., Corbis-Bettmann, Wide World

Edited by Lori Kinstad Pupeza
Contributing editor Brooke Henderson
Special thanks to our Checkerboard Kids—Kenny Abdo, Aisha Baker, Matthew Nichols

All statistics taken from the 1990 census; The Rand McNally Discovery Atlas of The United States. Other sources: *Connecticut*, Fradin and Fradin, Children's Press, Chicago, 1995; *Connecticut*, Kent, Children's Press, Chicago ,1990; *Connecticut*, Gelman, Lerner Publications Co., Minneapolis, 1991; America Online, Compton's Living Encyclopedia, 1997; World Book Encyclopedia, 1990.

Library of Congress Cataloging-in-Publication Data

Welsbacher, Anne, 1955-
    Connecticut / Anne Welsbacher.
    p. cm. -- (United States)
    Includes index.
    Summary: Examines the people, geography, history, and natural resources of the Constitution State.
    ISBN 1-56239-866-0
    1. Connecticut--Juvenile literature. [1. Connecticut.] I. Title. II. Series: United States (Series)
    F94.3.W44 1998
    974.6--DC21
                                   97-15207
                                   CIP
                                   AC

Contents

Welcome to Connecticut 4

Fast Facts About Connecticut............................... 6

Nature's Treasures 8

Beginnings 10

Happenings 12

Connecticut's People 18

Seaside Cities 20

Connecticut's Land 22

Connecticut at Play 24

Connecticut at Work 26

Fun Facts 28

Glossary 30

Internet Sites 31

Index 32

Welcome to Connecticut

Connecticut is a very small state. It is the third smallest state in the United States! But it plays a big part in the country.

Connecticut was one of the first states to join the United States. It helped decide important laws about how the United States would be run. And it was one of the first states to outlaw slavery.

Steamboats, the cotton gin, and the "six-shooter" gun were **invented** in Connecticut.

Many things are built today in Connecticut. They are clocks, airplane engines, knives, and tools for machines.

Opposite page: The steamboat was invented in Connecticut.

Fast Facts

CONNECTICUT

Capital
Hartford (139,739 people)
Area
4,872 square miles
(12,618 sq km)
Population
3,295,669 people
Rank: 27th
Statehood
Jan. 9, 1788
(5th state admitted)
Principal river
Connecticut River
Highest point
Mount Frissell;
2,380 feet (725 m)
Largest City
Bridgeport (141,686 people)
Motto
Qui transtulit sustinet
(He who transplanted still
sustains)
Song
"Yankee Doodle"
Famous People
Ethan Allen, P.T. Barnum,
Katharine Hepburn, Harriet
Beecher Stowe

Connecticut is one of the original 13 colonies
13

*M*ountain Laurel

*S*tate Flag

*W*hite Oak

*A*merican Robin

About Connecticut
The Constitution State

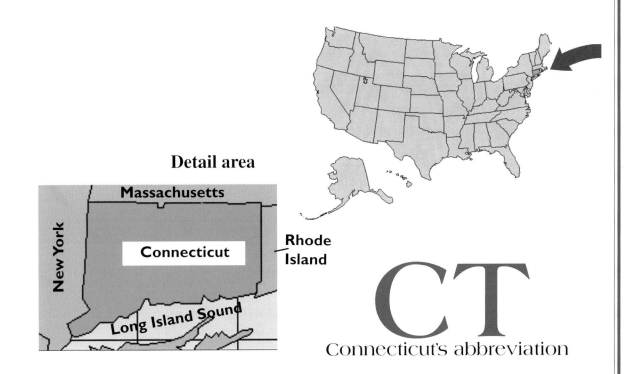

Detail area

Massachusetts

New York

Connecticut

Rhode Island

Long Island Sound

CT
Connecticut's abbreviation

Borders: west (New York), north (Massachusetts), east (Rhode Island), south (Long Island Sound)

Nature's Treasures

Connecticut has many trees. But they do not make good lumber. The soil does not have many **minerals**. The land is not good for farming.

The weather in Connecticut is not too hot and not too cold. It is just right! Connecticut gets about 25 inches (64 centimeters) of snow in a year. It rains about 47 inches (119 centimeters) in a year.

The Connecticut River is the biggest river in Connecticut. It cuts through the middle of the state. Other rivers that run through Connecticut are the Housatonic, Naugatuck, Shepaug, Thames, and Quinebaug. Connecticut has more than 1,000 lakes.

Opposite page: The Connecticut River.

Beginnings

About 10,000 years ago, Native Americans lived in Connecticut. Some of them were called the Algonquians. Others were the Nipmuc and Pequots. West of Connecticut were the Mohawks.

In the 1600s, Dutch and English people came. They traded with the Native Americans. But they also fought battles with them.

The English **claimed** Connecticut as a **colony**. The colonists wanted to start a new country. In 1776, Connecticut and other colonies signed the Declaration of Independence. It said they were a new country. Then they fought the Revolutionary War with England. The colonies won. They became the United States of America.

In 1788, Connecticut became the fifth state. It had one of the first written **constitutions**. So Connecticut is called the Constitution State.

In the 1800s, Connecticut had many **inventors**. They **invented** easier ways to make things. They made clocks, silk, bicycles, cigars, pins, needles, and rubber shoes!

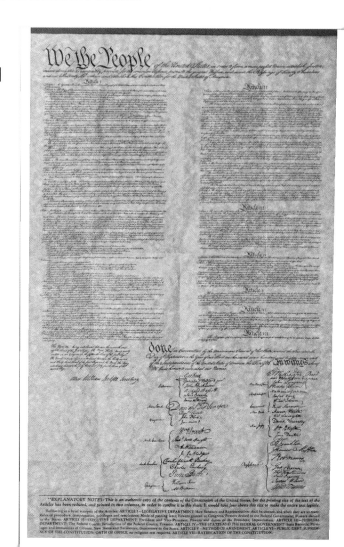

The United States Constitution, written by the forefathers of the United States.

B.C. to 1700s

Early Times

10,000 B.C.-1600s: Algonquians, Nipmuc, and Pequots live in Connecticut area.

1600s: Dutch and English traders arrive.

1637: The Pequot fight with other Native Americans and settlers.

1701: Yale University is founded.

Connecticut

B.C. to 1700s

1776 to 1788

A New Country

 1776: Connecticut and other states sign the Declaration of Independence.

 1784: Connecticut outlaws slavery.

 1788: Connecticut becomes the fifth state.

14

Connecticut
1776 to 1788

1833 to Today

Inventing the Future

 1833: A school for African-American girls is opened by Prudence Crandall.

 1833: Samuel Colt **invents** the revolver.

 1910: The United States Coast Guard Academy moves to Connecticut.

 1958: The Connecticut turnpike opens.

Connecticut

1833 to Today

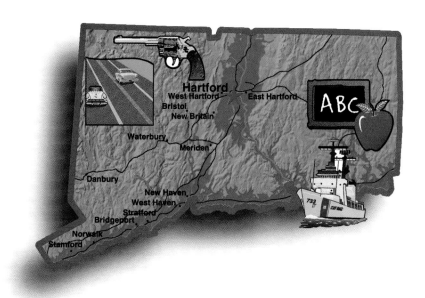

Connecticut's People

There are almost 3.3 million people in Connecticut. Almost everybody lives in a city. People in Connecticut are white, African American, Latino, Asian, and Native American.

Ralph Nader is from Connecticut. He works for safer cars and better **products**. The actress Katharine Hepburn was born in Hartford. The editor Clare Booth Luce also was from Connecticut.

Ice skater Dorothy Hamill is from Connecticut. She won her first skating championship at age 12. And the circus king, P.T. Barnum, came from Connecticut. He was also mayor of Bridgeport!

Other Connecticut-born people are the composer Charles Ives, leader Ella Grasso, and Samuel Colt, who **invented** the Colt revolver.

Katharine Hepburn

Dorothy Hamill

P.T. Barnum

Seaside Cities

Bridgeport is the largest city in Connecticut. It is in the south, near the ocean. Other cities by the sea are Norwalk and Stamford.

Hartford is the next largest city in Connecticut. It is also the capital. It is in the middle of the state.

New Haven is the third largest city. Yale, a well known college, is in New Haven. Also in Connecticut is the house where Mark Twain lived for 20 years, writing some of his best work ever. Other cities are Waterbury, and New Britain.

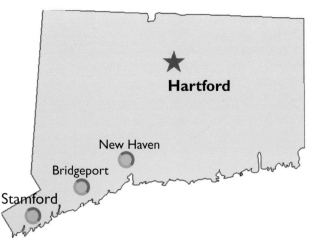

Opposite page:
Stamford, Connecticut.

20

Connecticut's Land

Connecticut is shaped like a rectangle with a tail that sticks out to the southwest. To the west is New York. To the north is Massachusetts. To the east is Rhode Island. To the south is Long Island sound, a **bay** off the Atlantic Ocean.

Connecticut has five land areas. The tiny Taconic section is at the top of the northwest corner. It has high mountains. Mountains are also part of the large western upland area.

The valley lowland is east of the mountains. It has many hills. The east side of the state is called the upland. It has many forests.

Along the bottom of the state are the coastal lowlands. This land lays next to the ocean. Many rivers flow into the ocean in this area.

There are many forests in Connecticut. They are filled with ash, beech, birch, oak, and pine trees. Connecticut animals are small. They are foxes, minks, otters, rabbits, and ducks. Birds like sparrows and warblers fly over Connecticut's land.

In the ocean waters are clams, lobsters, and oysters. Trout swim in Connecticut's many lakes.

Connecticut has mild weather. North Connecticut gets snow in the winter. Further south the state gets rain.

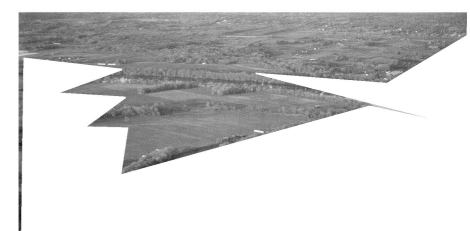

The Connecticut River cutting through farmland.

Connecticut at Play

Connecticut has many **historic** houses and parks. Putnam Memorial State Park is near Danbury. Many soldiers were held there during the Revolutionary War.

At Gillette Castle near Haddam is a strange-looking house. It is made of rocks and has a funny shape. One of the actors who played Sherlock Holmes lived there.

In Mystic, the Marinelife Aquarium has more than 6,000 kinds of sea creatures! Mystic Seaport has an old whaling ship in the **bay**.

There are many parks in Connecticut. In forests and hill areas, people can hike and ride horses. Near rivers, they can fish. In the winter, people ski on the snow-topped mountains. And in May, they enjoy the Dogwood Festival. When the dogwood trees bloom, people go on tours of pretty gardens.

Connecticut at Work

Many people living in Connecticut work in service. They cook and serve food, work in parks, and do other things for tourists who visit the state.

United Postal Service, called UPS, is based in Connecticut. Perhaps UPS has brought packages to your house!

Many people also work in **manufacturing**. Other people fish or work with the railroads. There are four railroads in Connecticut.

Many people sell houses and land. Or they work with money. For example, they help other people decide how much money to save or spend.

Some people farm. They raise chickens for eggs. And they grow many pretty flowers.

Many also work for newspapers. There are 80 newspapers in Connecticut! *The Connecticut Courant* began in 1764. It is the oldest newspaper in the country.

A chicken farm in Connecticut.

Fun Facts

• The first cookbook by an American came from Hartford, in 1796. Amelia Simmons wrote the book, called American Cookery.

• The football tackling dummy was **invented** at Yale University, in New Haven, in 1889. The man who invented it became a great football coach. His name was Amos Alonzo Stagg.

• For almost 200 years, Connecticut had two capital cities! They were Hartford and New Haven.

• The man who wrote the Webster dictionary, Noah Webster, was from Hartford, Connecticut.

• Airplane pilots flying over Connecticut at nighttime say they see almost no lights from the sky. This is different from almost all other states, which can be seen at night from the sky.

The football tackling dummy was invented in Connecticut.

Glossary

Bay: an area of the ocean near the land.

Claim: to take.

Colony: a place owned by another country.

Constitution: a set of laws written by the people, not a king.

Historic: something about history.

Invent: to make for the first time.

Inventor: a person who invents things.

Manufacture: to make or build things.

Minerals: a substance found in the earth like diamonds, coal, or gold, that is not a plant, an animal, or another living thing.

Products: things that people buy.

Internet Sites

CT Central
http://www.ctcentral.com
News, weather, sports, and entertainment information–updated hourly and fully searchable.

Connecticut Passport
http://www.ctpassport.com
From local fairs...to professional sporting events...to car shows...to theatrical events...it's all here at your fingertips... and it's all free!

These sites are subject to change. Go to your favorite search engine and type in Connecticut for more sites.

PASS IT ON

Tell Others Something Special About Your State

To educate readers around the country, pass on interesting tips, places to see, history, and little unknown facts about the state you live in. We want to hear from you!

To get posted on ABDO & Daughters website E-mail us at "mystate@abdopub.com"

Index

A

African-American 16
Algonquians 10, 12
Atlantic Ocean 22

B

Bridgeport 6, 18, 20

C

colony 10
Colt, Samuel 16, 18
Connecticut River 6, 8
constitution 11
cotton gin 4

D

Declaration of Indepen-
  dence 10, 14
Dutch 10, 12

E

English 10, 12

F

fish 24, 26
forests 22, 24

G

Gillette Castle 24

H

Hartford 6, 18, 20, 28

I

inventors 11

L

lumber 8

M

Marinelife Aquarium 24
Mohawks 10
mountains 22, 24
Mystic Seaport 24

N

Native Americans 10
New Haven 20, 28
New York 22
Norwalk 20

P

Pequots 10, 12

R

railroads 26
Revolutionary War 10, 24
river 6

S

settlers 12
six-shooter 4
slavery 4, 14
Stamford 20
steamboats 4

T

traders 12
Twain, Mark 20

U

United Postal Service 26
United States Coast Guard
  Academy 16

W

weather 8, 23

Y

Yale University 12, 28